Keys to Eliminate Negative Emotion:
A Guide on how to regulate your Emotions for better days

Kimberly Henry

Table of contents

Chapter 1

The truth about negative emotions

What are Negative Emotions?
It's crucial to differentiate between what an emotion is and what a feeling is. While the two are related, there's a wider distinction than you may assume. It's absolutely something that startled me when I started my investigation.

Emotions - Emotions are characterized as 'lower level' reactions. They initially arise in the subcortical parts of the brain such as the amygdala and the ventromedial prefrontal cortices. These regions are responsible for creating metabolic responses that have a direct influence on your physical condition.

Emotions are inscribed into our DNA and are considered to have evolved as a means to help us adapt swiftly to varied environmental hazards, much like our 'fight or flight response. The amygdala has also been proven to have a role in the production of neurotransmitters that are crucial for memory, which is why emotional memories are typically stronger and simpler to remember.

Emotions have a stronger physical basis than emotions meaning researchers find them simpler to detect scientifically via bodily signs such as blood flow, heart rate, brain activity, facial expressions, and body language.

Feelings - Emotions are considered as preceding feelings, which tend to be our responses to the diverse emotions we encounter. Where emotions may have a more generic experience across all people, feelings are more subjective and are impacted by our particular experiences and perceptions of our reality based on those experiences.

Feelings arise in the neocortical areas of the brain and are the next stage in how we react to our emotions as an individual. Because they are so subjective, they can't be quantified the way emotions can.

Psychologists have long examined the breadth of human emotions and their classifications. Eckman (1999) identified fundamental basic emotions:

Anger\Disgust
Fear
Happiness
Sadness
Surprise

He eventually built on this to add a further main emotions:

Amusement
Contempt\sContentment

Embarrassment
Excitement
Guilt\sPride\sRelief
Satisfaction
Sensory Pleasure
Shame

Pam (2013) describes negative emotions "as an unpleasant or sad feeling which is produced in persons to communicate a negative affect towards an event or person." It's very straightforward to distinguish those that may be referred to as 'negative' emotions.

While we may use the word negative, knowing what we know about emotions, it's crucial to understand that all feelings are natural to experience. They are a part of our entrenched DNA. What is more essential, is recognizing when and why negative emotions could occur, and creating constructive habits to overcome them.

A Look at the Psychology of Emotions
One of the most prominent psychological theories of emotions is Robert Plutchik's Wheel of Emotions. Plutchik (1980) argued that there are eight primary emotions: pleasure, trust, fear, surprise, sorrow, anticipation, anger, and disgust. Plutchik went further by combining the emotions with their opposites and then developing the wheel of emotions, which helps to elucidate on how intricate and interactive our emotions are.

Sadness is the antithesis of Joy
Anticipation is the opposite of Surprise
Anger is the antithesis of Fear
Disgust is the antithesis of Trust
Plutchik's wheel is a good visual illustration of how our emotions manifest themselves. As you can see the core feeling lowers as you travel outward on the wheel. Plutchik also employed the color to symbolize the strength of the emotion: the darker the hue,

the more powerful it is. So at its most strong trust becomes adoration, and at its least intense, acceptance.

They thought that our emotions offer us input about the safety of our surroundings and our aptitude to manage particular events. In this sense, unpleasant emotions give us the greatest indicator that something is not right, or that our safety could be endangered.

Anxiety is typically perceived as a bad feeling, yet it's an essential one to propel us to action. We frequently find it difficult to react to events without the presence of this feeling but it's crucial to keep it in control as continuous worry might impede our cognitive performance (Rosen, 2008).

Adler, Rosen, and Silverstein (1998) studied the influence of negative emotions on the role of bargaining. Focusing on two negative emotions — fear and anger — they discovered that negotiators who couldn't manage or comprehend these emotions when they occurred were typically unable to arbitrate the issue successfully, despite their training. A similar study has studied the ways various emotions, such as anger and thankfulness, alter cognition and behavior within the setting of mediation (Williams and Hinshaw, 2018)

Anger

Ever had someone tell you not to do something you want? How does it make you feel? Does your blood begin to boil, your temperature increase, and do you figuratively 'see red'? This is often how rage is characterized. Your body is responding to things not going your way, and it's an effort to try to remedy that.

Often when we're upset we'll yell, our face will show our displeasure and we may even toss things about. We're attempting to get our way in a circumstance and this is the only way we can imagine of. If you're regularly responding to events in this manner, it's a good idea to analyze why and come up with more constructive tactics.

Annoyance

Do you have a coworker who sometimes speaks too loudly? Does your lover constantly leave their dirty dishes in the sink? Though we may like our colleagues and adore our relationship these habits might make us feel incredibly frustrated. Referring to Pluchik's wheel, you can observe that irritation is the lesser form of rage.

While not as severe as anger, it's the outcome of a similar cognitive process: something has occurred or someone is doing something you wish they wouldn't. And you have no control over it.

Fear

Fear is typically mentioned as one of the fundamental basic emotions, and that's because it's intimately related to our sense of self-preservation. It's an evolutionary reaction to alert us about risky circumstances, unforeseen barriers, or failures. We don't sense fear to feel worried, on the contrary, it's there to assist us to handle possible risks effectively.

Embracing the feeling of dread and examining why it emerges might help you prepare yourself proactively to handle situations.

Anxiety

Much like fear, anxiety strives to alert us about possible hazards and dangers. It's typically considered a negative feeling since it's believed having an anxious temperament hinders judgment and our capacity to behave. A new study has revealed the reverse.

Sadness

When you miss a deadline, receive a terrible grade, or don't obtain the job you had your hopes fastened on, you'll probably feel depressed. Sadness may be wonderful to feel since it reveals to us that we are enthusiastic about something. It may be a tremendous impetus to seek change.

Guilt

Guilt is a difficult emotion. We may experience this in connection to ourselves and prior actions that we wish hadn't occurred, but also concerning how our conduct influences people around us. Guilt is sometimes referred to as a 'moral emotion' (Haidt, 2000) and maybe another powerful stimulus to inspire us to make changes in our lives.

Apathy

Like guilt, indifference may be a complicated feeling. If you've lost excitement, drive, or interest in the things you've previously loved, this might be connected to indifference. Like anger, it can arise when we lose control over a scenario or situation but instead of becoming angry, we pursue a more passive-aggressive expression of rebellion.

Despair
Ever tried to achieve a certain task or goal multiple times and not succeeded? Did it make you feel like throwing your hands in the air, and camping out in bed with a giant container of ice cream for a company? That's despair and it's a feeling that occurs when we aren't obtaining the outcomes we desire. Despair provides us an excuse to give up on our desired objectives and it comes back to a self-preservation approach.

Despair may be a beneficial reminder to take a pause and recover, before continuing to pursue a tough objective.

As a human being, you will experience a full range of emotions throughout your lifetime in response to rapidly changing situations. No emotion is without purpose. It's when we begin to further explore and understand the purpose behind each emotion, that we learn new ways to respond which supports our emotional growth and sense of well-being.

When studying unpleasant emotions, it's also crucial to remember that they are not the only source of knowledge you have access to. Before you act upon any emotion you should also seek to explore your previous experiences, stored knowledge, memories, personal values, and desired outcomes for any given scenario (Shpancer, 2010).

Chapter 2

How to control your emotions

Emotions can be a true minefield—they may be our best friend or our worst adversary. Some have a knack for creeping up on you when you least expect it and others prefer to stake out a comfy area in your brain and settle down for the long term.

These negative nasties are part of our emotional composition. You can't outrun them and you can't hide from them. Instead of being kept captive at their mercy each time they emerge, maybe a change in perspective is required. In attempting to understand their purpose and learning how to discharge them healthily, we may create a healthier connection with them so that they come up as overnight visitors instead of settling in for good.

Changing your emotional behavior is never simple, but here's how to regulate your emotions.

Changing the way you typically do anything is challenging, and it is much more difficult when it comes to emotions. When we are feeling "emotional," the last thing we want to do is calm down and attempt to deal with the matter proactively; we most commonly want to rant about what is troubling us.

If we understand a bit more about how our emotions function, we are in a much better position to utilize this knowledge to our benefit. Learning how to regulate your emotions might be one of the finest talents you will ever gain in your life. Your emotions lead to the behaviors you conduct and, therefore, create the life you are experiencing now—every component of it.

Our emotional section of the brain, the limbic system, is one of the oldest parts as compared, for example, to our prefrontal cortex, which is our 'thinking' part

The typical person's emotional section of the brain is nearly six billion times more active than the prefrontal cortex. Because our emotional component is so old and is an extraordinarily powerful part of the brain, it is logical that it seems like our emotions periodically dominate us.

The point is, your emotions will naturally hijack your thinking—this is a given—but there are still strategies to cope with this.

Ignoring emotions, repressing them, or not dealing with them will come back to harm you! Stress and anxiety arise from repressed emotions, therefore if you believe that dealing with your emotions by ignoring them is going to help, you are sadly incorrect.

Here are techniques to regulate your emotions properly.

1. Awareness
If you are not conscious of the moments when you are too emotional or overreacting, how can you attempt to moderate it? It is impossible.
If we refuse to deal with them, they find a hiding spot deep within our bodies. Stuffing our sentiments down by pretending they don't exist or lying to ourselves merely prolongs the process.

Instead, when you sense a bad emotion creeping in, attempt to genuinely sit with it for a time. It is no simple undertaking and may be quite intense initially. Notice which part of your body it's affecting, and then name the emotion. In saying out loud, "I'm feeling anxious right now," it can loosen its grip.

2. Discover the 'Why' of Your Emotions
Once you have defined how you are feeling, you want to uncover why you are experiencing it. What is producing this emotion within you? Of course, there may be a million causes, and to find out you have to ask yourself, as you would a friend, "What is wrong? What is driving me to feel this way? " Your mind will constantly hunt for a solution.

Most of the time, just the way you are thinking about the circumstance is leading you to feel the way you do. Another big reason why we experience unpleasant emotions is that our ideals are not present at that time or are not being honored.

Remember: uncover the 'why.'

3. Ask Yourself, "What Is the Solution? "
Once you have found why, what can you do to take back control? Sometimes, you may need to adjust your ideas about the circumstance.

Your ideas go straight to your emotions; hence if you are feeling unpleasant, you most certainly have negative thinking making you feel that way. If you approach the matter from a new aspect, you will begin to feel better instantly. What you concentrate on increases!

Sometimes, knowing why you feel a specific way at the moment, might make your feelings fade. This is because knowing always leads to tranquility.

4. Choose How You Want to React

This is the toughest part. The way we respond and control our emotions is a habit. Haven't you observed that those who get worried over everything, practically panic out about nothing? You almost feel sorry for them. They have formed a habit of linking a circumstance they don't like with "freaking out." Their emotions have hijacked them.

Learning to listen to your emotions, to recognize, understand, and then select them, isn't something that you decide to do twice a week at lunchtime. No, it needs ongoing work and dedication to cultivate this crucial talent.

5. Ritualize Your Mornings

Have you ever gone to bed furious and woken up with the same fury burning a hole in your pillow? Or just woken up on the wrong side of the bed, feeling awful for no apparent reason. The first few seconds of the morning might be one of the most powerful. Whatever attitude we crawl out of bed in seems to stick to us all day. That's why it may be so beneficial to establish a morning routine to wash the emotional palette. Effective rituals vary, however, the following may be particularly effective:

Meditation

Quieting the mind with breath is simply one of the most powerful weapons we have to release bad feelings, however, it is no simple job.

Find a peaceful area and sit silently for ten to fifteen minutes, concentrating on your breath or on a mantra (I find inhaling "Let" and expelling "Go" to be simple but powerful). When we build a meditation practice, our monkey mind learns to calm and we become more in touch with ourselves, in turn leading to awareness.

Being mindful creates more space between our thoughts so that we can be aware when negative emotions creep in, allowing us to nip it in the bud before the emotion snowballs and takes over your day or your week.

6. Massage for Relaxation and to Empty the Mind.

Have you ever intensively concentrated on something for a long time and then unconsciously reached up to rub the back of your neck? Massage decreases anxiety and pressure and revives both the body and the mind, providing more clarity and focus.

Because it affects both the mind and the body, it fosters a sense of well-being, thereby relieving a negative mood.

7. Exorcize Through Exercise
As human beings, we are created to move. Exercise is helpful for us not just from a physical standpoint but from a mental one. The hormones released when our hearts are pumping and our bodies are moving can change our mindset.

The sheer act of going for a walk, a run, or hitting a set of weights compels the mind to concentrate on the job at hand. Next time something enrages you, instead of grabbing for a bag of chips or numbing out in front of the TV, get physical. Even if it means dancing about your room like crazy to some gangster rap music (a particular favorite of mine), you'll feel a heck better and perhaps have a giggle at just how goofy you look.

Final Thoughts
Do you control emotions, or do they control and lead you?

It's not simple, and that is why so many individuals make little effort or quit. But once you can control your emotions, life changes for you in more ways than you ever dreamed possible. Not only will you feel way more empowered and in control in life, but you will be happier and much healthier as you won't be stressed or weighed down so often.

Chapter 3

Developing a positive thoughts

Positive thinking may be attained by several different approaches that have been shown helpful, such as positive self-talk and positive imagery.

Here are some techniques to get you started that may help you educate your brain on how to think positively.

Focus on the nice things
Challenging conditions and hurdles are a part of life. When you're presented with one, concentrate on the positive things no matter how tiny or trivial they appear. If you seek it, you can always discover the proverbial silver lining in every cloud – even if it's not immediately evident. For example, if someone cancels plans, concentrate on how

it frees up time for you to catch up on a TV program or other activity you like.

Practice gratitude
Practicing thankfulness has been demonstrated to lower stress, boost self-esteem, and develop resilience even in extremely tough situations. Think about individuals, events, or things that provide you some type of comfort or enjoyment, and attempt to show your thanks at least once a day. This may be thanking a co-worker for assisting with a project, a loved one for doing the dishes, or your dog for the unconditional love they provide you.

Keep a gratitude journal
writing down the things you're thankful for might increase your optimism and feeling of well-being. You may do this by writing in a thankfulness diary every day, or scribbling

down a list of things you're grateful for on days you're having a hard time.

Open oneself open to comedy
Studies have indicated that laughing decreases stress, anxiety, and sadness. It also enhances coping skills, mood, and self-esteem.

Be receptive to comedy in all circumstances, even the unpleasant ones, and allow yourself permission to chuckle. It quickly lightens the atmosphere and makes things seem a bit less challenging. Even if you're not feeling it; faking or pushing yourself to laugh might enhance your mood and lessen stress.

Spend time with positive individuals
Negativity and optimism have been proven to be infectious. Consider the folks with whom you're spending time. Have you

noticed how someone in a poor mood can pull down practically everyone in a room? A positive person has the opposite influence on others.

Being around positive individuals has been proven to promote self-esteem and raise your chances of accomplishing objectives. Surround yourself with individuals who will raise you and help you see the bright side.

Practice positive self-talk
We tend to be the harshest on ourselves and be our own worst critics. Over time, this might lead you to acquire a poor impression of yourself that can be hard to shake. To stop this, you'll need to be mindful of the voice in your head and respond with positive messages, also known as positive self-talk.

Identify your areas of negativity
Take a thorough look at the numerous aspects of your life and identify the ones in which you tend to be the most negative. Not sure? Ask a trustworthy friend or coworker. Chances are, they'll be able to provide some insight. A co-worker could notice that you tend to be pessimistic at work. Your partner may notice that you become unusually negative when driving. Tackle one region at a time.

Positive thinking isn't about hiding every bad thought or emotion you have or avoiding tough sensations. The lowest periods in our life are frequently the ones that drive us to go on and make great changes.

When going through such a moment, try to perceive yourself as if you were a dear friend in need of comfort and sensible guidance. What would you say to her? You'd likely accept her sentiments and tell her she has every right to feel sad or upset in her circumstances, and then give support with a gentle reassurance that things will get better.

Chapter 4

Positive Self Affirmation

Favorable affirmations had a positive impact on persons with high self-esteem but a negative effect on people with low self-esteem. The researchers discovered that persons with existing low levels of self-esteem who produced present-tense ("I am...") positive affirmations ended up feeling worse than people who made positive comments but were also permitted to evaluate ways in which the assertions may be false.

Think of this as a menu of alternatives. Each morning, immediately upon awakening, choose a handful and repeat them out loud and/or write them down. Doing this will set the tone for your day and start you going in a good manner.

I am successful.

I am confident.
I am powerful.
I am strong.
I am growing better and better every day.
All I need is inside me right now.
I wake up inspired.
I am an unstoppable force of nature.
I am; an alive, breathing example of a drive.
I am living with wealth.
I am having a good and inspirational influence on the individuals I come into touch with.
I am motivating others through my work.
I'm rising above the ideas that are attempting to make me furious or terrified.
Today is a wonderful day.
I am dialing DOWN the level of negativity in my life, while simultaneously cranking UP the volume of optimism.
I am full of attention.
I am not driven by my troubles; I am guided by my aspirations.
I am thankful for all I have in my life.
I am independent and self-sufficient.

I can be anything I want to be.

I am not defined by history; I am motivated by my future.

I utilize adversities to inspire me to study and improve.

Today will be a productive day.

I am clever and focused.

I feel more thankful each day.

I am becoming healthier every day.

Every day, I am coming closer to reaching my objectives.

Through the power of my ideas and words, great shifts are occurring in me and within my life right now.

I am continually improving and expanding into a better person.

I'm releasing myself from any damaging uncertainty and dread.

I accept myself for who I am and develop calm, power, and confidence in my mind and heart.

I am going to forgive myself and release myself. I deserve to forgive and be forgiven.

I am healing and stronger every day.

I've made it through bad times before, and I've come out stronger and better because of them. I'm going to make it through this.

I do not throw away a single day of my life. I squeeze every ounce of worth out of each of my days on this planet—today, tomorrow, and every day.

I must remember the amazing strength I hold inside me to accomplish everything I wish.

I do not connect with folks who attempt to pierce my head with destructive thoughts and ideas—I walk away when a person or a circumstance isn't healthy for me.

I belong in this world; some individuals care about me and my value.

My history could be nasty, but I am still lovely.

I have made errors, but I will not let them define me.

My spirit emanates from the inside and warms the souls of others.

I don't compare myself to others. The only person I compare myself to is the person I was yesterday. And as long as the person I am today is even the least bit better than the person I was yesterday—I'm reaching my definition of success.

Note to self: I am going to make you very proud.

I complete what counts and let go of what does not.

I nourish my spirit. I train my physique. I concentrate on my thoughts. This is my moment.

My life has significance. What I do has a purpose. My acts are significant and inspirational.

What I have done today was the best I was able to accomplish today. And for that, I am grateful.

One simple optimistic thought in the morning may affect my entire day. So, today I wake with a strong idea to set the tone and enable success to resonate through every minute of my day.

I create objectives and go for them with all the tenacity I can manage. When I accomplish this, my abilities and talents will lead me to areas that astound me.

Happiness is a decision, and today I choose to be happy.

For Your Thoughts

Thoughts, listen up! Stop being so dispersed. Stop spending your time and energy with anxieties, doubts, worries, and old memories that don't do us any good. From now on I want you to think of good, strong, purpose-driven ideas. Think about love. Think of attractive and inspirational things. Think about how we'll conquer our hurdles and demolish our ambitions. Think about our vision for the future and our preparations for realizing it. Think about assisting others and contributing to the larger good. Think of fresh concepts. Think about ways of improving. Think exclusively about ideas that I can utilize to develop myself. If any other ideas come along, look at them, throw them out, and go back to productive thoughts.

For Your Emotions

Emotions, listen up! Stop concentrating on concerns and anxieties, the pain and troubles from the past. Stop hanging on to wrath, guilt, resentment, envy, and similar feelings. When any of these emotions occur, go ahead and experience those sentiments for a short while, and then let them fly away and replace them with empowered ones. I want you to focus on empowered emotions, successful sentiments, pleasant feelings, joyful feelings, confident feelings, loving feelings, and sensations filled with optimism. I want you to experience these types of feelings as frequently as possible going ahead.

For Your Body

Body, listen up! You are great, and you do all sorts of beautiful things like pump blood through my body, replace and regenerate my cells, and enable my heart to beat over a hundred thousand times a day — all without me ever having to instruct you to do so. But now I want you to do everything even better. I want you to enhance our energy. I want you to strengthen our strength. I want you to increase our health in every possible way so that we do everything at the highest level and maintain a perpetual state of peak performance. It's time to be even more competent and elegant in whatever you do, to use every ounce of food and air even more efficiently than you currently do, and to quit any behaviors that hinder our power, energy, vitality, and health. And the body, I want you to relax more, experience pleasure more, enjoy life more, and provide greater pleasure to others.

Thank You
Thank you Thoughts, thank you Emotions, thank you Body, thank you for being the unstoppable force of nature that I am!

www.ingramcontent.com/pod-product-compliance
Lightning Source LLC
Chambersburg PA
CBHW071500150726
48000CB00006B/2642